The Best Songs Come at Night

The Best Songs Come at Night

and Other Christmas Proverbs

An Advent Study for Adults

J. Ellsworth Kalas

Abingdon Press
Nashville

THE BEST SONGS COME AT NIGHT
AND OTHER CHRISTMAS PROVERBS

Library of Congress Cataloging-in-Publication Data

Kalas, J. Ellsworth, 1923–
   The best songs come at night : and other Christmas proverbs : an Advent study for adults / J. Ellsworth Kalas.
      p.   cm.
   ISBN 978-0-687-65980-7 (binding: pbk., saddle-stitched 2-wires : alk. paper) 1. Advent—Meditations. I. Title.
   BV40.K335   2009
242'.332—dc22

2009013895

09 10 11 12 13 14 15 16 17 18—10 9 8 7 6 5 4 3 2 1

MANUFACTURED IN THE UNITED STATES OF AMERICA

Contents

Preface

Somehow we don't usually associate wisdom with the Advent and Christmas seasons. True, Advent should by its description be a thoughtful time, since it is meant to prepare us to celebrate the coming of our Lord. But the mood all around us, from decorations to wrapping paper to social gatherings to the music in the malls, is celebrative rather than thoughtful. For many people, the weeks leading to Christmas are more of a frenetic escape than a call to thoughtful contemplation.

In this study, however, I want us to enter into the wisdom of the season. It's rather simple wisdom, as you will soon see. But as most of us slowly learn, important wisdom tends to be quite basic, which is probably why it is so hard to master.

And of course it is appropriate that wisdom coming from the Christmas scene should be simple and unadorned. A baby being born in a manger-cave—no obstetrician present, no nurses, no hospital machinery: what could be simpler?

The aphorisms that title our four chapters may sound familiar. They seemed so to me when I began developing this little book. I have no idea where they originated. Perhaps, for instance, it was Eve (or even

Adam) who first said, "Miracles begin as babies." But we've been delving into the truth of these little wisdoms through every generation, and we still haven't plumbed their depths or touched their heights.

I have enjoyed preparing this study for you. I pray that you will be blessed in your reading, contemplating, and discussing.

J. Ellsworth Kalas

Miracles Begin as Babies

Scripture: Read Matthew 1:18-25

God had a problem. One of the planets, Earth, hadn't turned out the way God had hoped it would. Still worse, according to the Bible, this was God's favorite planet. It's far from the biggest, and the other planets don't revolve around it, but it's obviously very special. Space travelers have given a vigorous supporting vote to this point of view, telling us that our planet is like a luxurious green jewel among the hurtling inhabitants of space, a uniquely favored spot.

But Earth had gone wrong. We human beings, the resident managers who had been entrusted with the care of Earth, had rebelled against God, and thus the loveliest of planets had become an occupied territory so that instead of operating on God's plan of love and holiness it was doing quite the opposite. For all practical purposes, Earth had sold out to the enemy. Now how was God to bring this erring planet back to himself, before it self-destructed?

God's answer was to make a benevolent invasion. But of course *benevolent invasion* is an oxymoron, invented by tyrants who want to force their will upon a people who haven't the power to resist them. An invasion, by common definition, means a show of force. Think of an invasion and you picture armaments, with the weaker unit bending unwillingly to the stronger. Of course God, being God, has the power to do that sort of thing, and I suppose you can say that God, being God, has the right to do whatever pleases him. After all, if this was God's planet in the first place, isn't it God's right to lay hold of it again, whatever the method?

But God didn't unleash a lesson in power. There was no exercise of divine rights. Nor did God marshal an overpowering angelic force or split the earth with a monstrous quake or erupt Vesuvius-like but on a grander scale in ten thousand mountains. There wasn't even a sky-shattering roll of thunder. God made a benevolent invasion. God sent a baby.

Can you think of a humbler, more artless, less threatening way of moving into our world? Yes, and more than that: can you think of a more *ordinary* way of doing so? This kind of entry happens thousands of times a day in every part of the world. This is the means by which every human creature enters our planet. What could be less suspect, less epochal, and more routine than the birth of a child? If God intended to make a benevolent invasion, this was surely it, because there couldn't be a more ordinary, less-threatening way.

But there's still more. God not only invaded Earth through a baby, God chose the humblest kind of entrance for that baby. The parents were poor peasant folk from Nazareth. City dwellers thought that people from that region "talked funny," just as people sometimes say today of people from isolated regions. But what would you expect of a child born to a village carpenter and his teenage bride?

And the baby was born in an unlikely place. Babies sometimes are. We wish every baby could be born in the antiseptic security of a modern hospital, but still today a majority of the world's infants come into the world in quite different circumstances. Some are born in places where, logic says, babies ought not to be born. They're born in camps for displaced persons, and during times of war they're born in relocation centers. Babies are born to women in prison and to poor souls in the throes of drug addiction in filthy, vermin-infested back rooms where you feel that you enter at peril of your life.

Well, some of you know the story well enough to remember that this baby was born in a cave, in back of an unrated hotel. No doubt some sheep and goats were in the cave, too, and the air was heavy with the smells of nature. It was no place for a baby to be born! It was an even more unlikely place for God to invade planet Earth.

"How silently, how silently, / the wondrous gift is given!" So Phillips Brooks wrote in "O Little Town of Bethlehem" as he recalled his own Christmas visit to Bethlehem. Just so silently did God begin the divine campaign to win back planet Earth.

Madeleine L'Engle, the remarkable novelist, essayist, and poet, put it this way:

> This is the irrational season
> When love blooms bright and wild.
> Had Mary been filled with reason
> There'd have been no room for the child.
> (Madeleine L'Engle, *The Irrational Season*
> [New York: Seabury Press, 1977], 27)

God became utterly vulnerable by approaching our Earth as a child. The ancient Greeks thought that a divine creature should be impassive—that is, unable to feel pain or to be affected by anything in the creation. The Bible portrays God in quite the opposite fashion, as one so anxious to win our world and so solicitous of our welfare as to pursue us. How astonishing an idea that the God of the universe would go on the hunt for us human creatures, and not simply for the human race as a whole but for any and all of us as individuals. If there is any question in your mind as to your worth, or for that matter, the worth of any other human, here is the answer from the only judge that matters, God: God *wants* us. Wants us enough to pursue us. If that be so, Ms. L'Engle's word is right: this is the *irrational* season because it is the season that reminds us that God desires these sometimes faltering, sometimes absurd, often irresponsible creatures and goes to irrational lengths to get us.

It's clear that sometimes we don't appreciate God's pursuit. When that ancient soul, Job, was at a peak of suffering, he complained that he wanted God to leave him alone long enough that he could swallow his spittle (Job 7:19). We sometimes grow weary of God's pursuit of us so that, in the language of the poet Francis Thompson, we "[flee] Him, down the nights and down the days." Human beings turn 'round to curse God—sometimes in anger because the divine law gets in our way, sometimes in pain because we think we've been treated unfairly, and sometimes in thoughtlessness because we hardly bother to think whose name we use. We wouldn't dare act so with a God who used his power maliciously and carelessly, but it's easy for human beings to be arrogant with a God who will be so vulnerable as to come to Earth as a baby.

But if we are sometimes arrogant with such a generous, sensitive Lord, it is also true that such a God appeals to the best in us. And that's the point of God's approach. God humbles himself selflessly to seek us by love so that when at last we come to him we will be love-disciples. We follow God, in Jesus Christ, not because we have been beaten into submission but because we have been loved back into the divine family. If any chains are holding us, they are the chains of love. So while God has become vulnerable to the point of rejection by entering our Earth through the helplessness of a baby, God has also appealed to the best in us. When we turn to such a God, we turn to him with our best, with readiness to love not only God but to love the rest of our human race as well.

You realize of course, as I do, that there is always more power in a baby than anyone can ever estimate. Any baby. Now mind you, from a physical point of view, we humans are the weakest of all creatures at birth and infancy because we are so completely dependent upon the care of others, and remain so dependent for so much longer than other creatures.

Yet a baby's power is awesome. Go to a maternity ward at visiting hours and see how parents and grandparents, aunts, uncles, and assorted friends press close to see a half-hidden and (in truth) rather nondescript little face. See how strangers stop to converse with someone who is tending a tiny baby. There are instances, of course, where some people brutalize an infant, but the horror we feel when we hear such a story only demonstrates further how deeply we revere babies and how powerful they are.

You never know what's wrapped up in a baby. I suspect that when Johann Sebastian Bach was born in 1685 the neighbors congratulated his parents on still another child and thought little more; certainly they didn't anticipate that more than three centuries later this baby would be seen as the primary exemplar of Christian and classical music. I remember a newspaper cartoon from my youth, titled simply "February 12, 1809." Two frontiersmen are talking in a country store. The one asks, "Anything special happen today?" to which the other replies, "Not much. I hear that Tom and Nancy Lincoln have had a son." You never know when a mother takes one more deep breath, pushes hard, and a baby gasps for its first exterior air that this infant may someday write a symphony, find a cure for cancer, or save a soul.

So in one sense of the word, the story of God's pursuing our human race through a baby is altogether logical. Everything that happens on our planet seems to depend eventually, from a human point of view, on babies. But it's quite another matter that God would compress the power and the future of the universe into such a vulnerable vehicle. The Apostle Paul saw the wonder of this process and marveled that Christ who

> was in the form of God,
>
> . . . .
>
> emptied himself,
>> taking the form of a slave,
>> being born in human likeness,

so he could suffer "death on a cross" (Philippians 2:6-8).

No doubt some would ask if such a story bears a hearing in our intellectually and scientifically sophisticated age. We know so much more now about mathematics, physics, medicine, economics, and varieties of science for which we didn't even have a name a century or two ago. Have we perhaps grown beyond this childlike Christmas story?

Our problems are so much more complex too. This planet of ours has always had conflict, whether with stones, arrows, or ammunition. But now we've perfected (if I may use that word!) munitions to a point where we can destroy tens of thousands of lives (perhaps even millions) in one act—and leave our planet polluted for generations to come. And there's starvation: it has always been a threat because of drought and other vagaries of weather. But now, in a time when transportation means that the fresh fruit or vegetables on our table may have been grown several thousand miles away, and when we seem equipped to conquer starvation by the tools of our genius, instead millions starve because of a demonic combination of political, economic, and military forces. Crimes of lust are as old as the human race; now lust is a guest in our family rooms through television or in the privacy of our offices through the Internet.

In light of such words as these, a tough-minded critic might well say, "We're no longer living in Bethlehem. Ours is a world of computers and high-powered systems, not a world of camels and shepherds. As for angels, if there are any, why don't they make an appearance now, when we need them so much?"

I hear this critic, but I have to answer him in my venue rather than his because I'm quite sure that our problems won't be solved by still more armaments, still more cleverness, or still more carefully orchestrated projects. Let us use our skills for all that they're worth, but let's keep our eyes open for miracles, because they still happen, and more often than not they begin small. Who knows what little idea, what modest program, what simple effort may become God's instrument of blessing? Miracles begin as babies: artless, deceptively simple, seemingly helpless—yet from them springs all that we know of the future, of hope and love and promise.

Charles Wesley was a theologian, a poet, and a father. With his brother John he began a movement that, worldwide, is one of the largest Christian bodies, though it is the youngest among major Christian movements. He operated comfortably in several languages. We remember him most for the thousands of hymns he wrote—or more particularly for the several that are sung in every Christian body, Protestant or Catholic.

Wesley hymns (so many of them composed on horseback, literally on the run) are often quite simple and direct. But as a trained theologian and philosopher, Charles Wesley knew that there is a cosmic struggle in our world between good and evil and that we human beings are caught in its toils. That's a despairing word, especially in times when we find ourselves or our generation in what seem to be hopeless dilemmas.

But Wesley also knew that God has sent a Savior, Jesus Christ, and that this Savior came as a baby. As a father, Wesley had looked often at infant hands. One day the poet, the theologian, and the father came together in Charles Wesley as he pondered the wonder of God's miracle at Bethlehem in "Join, All Ye Joyful Nations":

> Gaze on that helpless Object
> Of endless adoration!
> Those infant hands
> Shall burst our bands,
> And work out our salvation:
>
> Strangle the crooked serpent,
> Destroy his works for ever,
> And open set
> The heavenly gate
> To every true believer.

I don't want to trivialize the massive problems of our time by easy sentiment. I do want us to remember, however, that in the daily run of our lives most of our pain comes from little hurts and slights and that correspondingly most of our healing comes from little kindnesses and timely words.

I dare also to submit that a great deal of the world's beauty is born in hidden places (like Emily Dickinson's poetry) and that a surprising number of our most significant scientific discoveries (like penicillin) emerge in unlikely places and that many financial empires begin in garages and back rooms—which is to say, never despise the day of small things.

But most of all, I want to say a theological word, a word of faith. And it is the ultimate Christmas word, the word about this season that goes beyond tinsel and trappings, parties and singing, cards and presents, and delightful times with families and friends. It is this: that God so loved our world as to pursue it—most particularly, its human inhabitants, in whose hands all the rest of the destiny of the planet is held. And God chose to pursue our human race in what was both the most artless and the most persuasive way. God came to our planet as a baby.

In doing so, God became vulnerable. The Apostle Paul said that our Lord

> emptied himself,
>> taking the form of a slave,
>> being born in human likeness. (Philippians 2:7)

Ultimately, he "became obedient to the point of death— / even death on a cross" (2:8). And the aim, quite simply, was to win the human race back to its original beauty—and indeed, more, because now the beauty was redeemed by the love of God brought to Earth in Jesus Christ.

So the Christmas story goes on, every day and every hour and every minute: every time, that is, that another human life turns from waywardness to God. It is an utterly astonishing miracle that has been going on for roughly two millennia, without a pause. And it all began with a baby.

Study Questions

1. What does Advent mean to you? Why is it important?
2. Describe some ways in which God's invasion was a benevolent one. Why was it necessary?
3. Why is God's pursuit of us often not appreciated?
4. Reflect on / discuss the role that love plays in God's plan for us.
5. Explain why *faith* is the ultimate Christmas word.
6. What lessons about miracles can be learned from this chapter?

Prayer

Dear God, thank you for the season of Advent. Help us see and appreciate all the miracles around us. Show us the real meaning of Christmas and guide us forward in love and in faith. Amen.

Focus for the Week

Begin your observance of Advent by counting all the miracles that touch your life each day. Reflect on past miracles and dream of future miracles God has waiting for you.

The Best Songs Come at Night

Scripture: Read Luke 2:8-18

It's only proper, I suppose, that I begin this chapter with a disclaimer: I am highly prejudiced toward music in general, and toward the music of the Christian faith in particular. And because I have an ear not only for melody and rhythm but also for words, my special passion in church music is that which brings together melody and text in strong and winsome combination.

My boyhood was blessed in many ways, but especially in that everyone in my family sang. My mother sang quite well and my father and my four sisters not only carried a tune but harmonized easily. Somehow we had a piano. This is surprising since the rest of our furniture was dreadfully basic. No one in our family played the piano, so I'm not sure why my parents at some time long before my appearance bought the instrument. But my mother did something that she called "chording," and one could sing very well with such leadership.

But I repeat my disclaimer: I am a prejudiced witness because I love music—especially the music of the church.

And as for Christmas and music: well, you can't really imagine Christmas without it. Our increasingly secular society is slowly pushing the faith-music of Christmas aside with songs of unsupported sentiment, yet even the most pagan souls in our culture eventually want to hear "Silent Night" or "Hark! The Herald Angels Sing."

As I read and reread the Christmas story, and as I sing the songs of the season, I offer a Christmas proverb: *The best songs come at night.* Songs are born in all kinds of times and circumstances and places, but the songs that live from generation to generation seem so often to have been born at night.

So let's think again on the familiar scene found in our Scripture for this week. The words take on a life of their own from some memory—perhaps the voice of a childhood priest or pastor or Sunday school teacher, or perhaps the voice from *A Charlie Brown Christmas.* Shepherds were in a field, keeping watch over their flocks by night. The air was biting cold, as the air would be in that season in semiarid country, and the men were weary. Although shepherding was not strenuous work, it was demanding and tiring on the best of days because you dared not to neglect your charges for even a few minutes. Nights were especially difficult. The greatest threat from hoodlum bands was always at night, and of course it was also at night that the wild animals were most likely to attack the flock. So no matter how tired a shepherd might be by the toils of the day, he had to be attentive to the unique concerns of the nighttime hours.

We can only imagine what was on the minds of these shepherds that fabled, historic night, and come to think of it, I suspect millions of people have engaged in such imagining—for that matter, these imaginings have appeared in poems, plays, Christmas pageants, and sermons without end. This we know: while the shepherds watched, they were interrupted by a personal invitation to explore a grand event, the birth of a unique baby in Bethlehem. Then, following the invitation, a multitude of the heavenly host reinforced the word of the angelic messenger with the loveliest of songs:

> Glory to God in the highest heaven,
>> and on earth, peace among those whom he favors! (Luke 2:14)

Perhaps it was only by chance that this song came to the shepherds during the night. But if it was just chance, the timing was surely symbolically significant. How appropriate that the song of hope—the greatest song of the greatest hope our planet will ever know—should burst upon earth in the darkness of night! It is in the darkest hours that we need songs the most, and it is in the night that the best songs are born.

Centuries earlier the prophet Isaiah said it would be so. He promised that the Messiah would come in the world's dark night.

> The people who walked in darkness
>> have seen a great light;
> those who lived in a land of deep darkness—
>> on them light has shined.
> . . . .
> For a child has been born for us,
>> a son given to us;
> authority rests upon his shoulders;
>> and he is named
> Wonderful Counselor, Mighty God,
>> Everlasting Father, Prince of Peace. (Isaiah 9:2, 6)

How dark was the world into which Jesus was born? One might cite all kinds of data. Personally, I find the most persuasive description in the words of that masterful twentieth-century Russian novelist, Boris Pasternak. The world, Pasternak said, was a "flea market of borrowed gods and conquered peoples, a bargain basement on two floors"

(*Dr. Zhivago* [New York: Pantheon, 1958], 43). The world was, indeed, a kind of bargain basement where the cheapest commodity was human life. Slavery, for instance: it is altogether possible that slavery was more pervasive at that time than at any period of human history. Consider, too, the contempt for the elements of society who were least able to defend themselves—those with physical limitations, the aged, children, and the poor. There was peace in the broad reaches of the Roman Empire, but it was an enforced peace, maintained by occupying armed forces.

But it would be irresponsible to identify that first-century world as "the worst" or to suggest that Christ came at that time because the world was more in need then than at any other time. Human need exists in every generation, and it would be very difficult to measure one generation against another on any scale of tragedy. Open the book of human history to any page and you will see our need of a Savior. The profile of our need changes in some particulars from generation to generation and from one part of the globe to another, but the need is always there. Sometimes its outline is more poignant or marked by more severe instances of human brutality or natural disaster. But ultimately our need seems to be built into our very humanness. It is the most certain inheritance bequeathed to us by our ancestors and our surest legacy to our descendants.

So Jesus came in the world's night, and there was a song, an angelic song. And the best songs come at night.

Much of Christendom follows a special calendar, and a great many congregations build their worship patterns around that calendar. The church calendar begins not with January 1 but with what we call the Advent season—four Sundays preceding Christmas Day that are intended to prepare us both as individual believers and as congregations for the coming of Christ. There is a section of music in most hymnals for this season, including such relatively familiar songs as "O Come, O Come, Emmanuel" and "Come, Thou Long-Expected Jesus."

Many congregations restrict their Advent music entirely to such hymns and postpone singing any of the traditional Christmas music until Christmas Day and the Sundays immediately following, the Sundays of Christmastide. I confess that I have mixed feelings about this practice. As Christians, we are a post-Christmas, not a pre-Christmas, people. Mind you, we do well to recall what the world was like without Christ and to understand the human longing with which the greatest souls waited for his coming. But we do still better to rejoice in what life is like as a result of Christ's coming.

I should also note that another emphasis of the Advent season, theologically, is on the second coming of Christ in his triumphant return. I fear that few worshipers grasp this part of the Advent message, partly because our preaching does not lift it up. Indeed, the larger message of the coming of Christ's kingdom deserves emphasis all through the year, in a variety of ways, rather than isolating it to a single, brief season.

Let me suggest a further quality for the music of Advent. I think at this moment of a particularly fine F. Melius Christiansen anthem, "Lost in the Night." It is an exquisite classical treatment of the Advent theme, describing the state of the world and the human soul without Christ. It ought, indeed, to be sung and celebrated. But I submit that the Advent repertoire ought to also include an anthem on the theme "*Found in the Night.*" For not only is it theologically true that our human race has been lost in the night of sin, it is also theologically and experientially right to rejoice that we have been found or, at the least, to note that the Finder has come to pursue us in our lostness, by way of the love demonstrated in Bethlehem and Calvary.

But grand as is the theme of the salvation of our human race, when we think of songs in the night many of us envision something smaller and closer at hand, but poignantly real. As a boy growing up in the Great Depression, I sat among poor people every Sunday morning and evening, probably half of them on government relief and many others wondering how soon they might find themselves in the same straits. I remember their singing prayer choruses that reassured them that Jesus would never fail; heaven and earth might pass away, but Jesus would never fail them. It was their song in the night, and it sustained them. It was strength to go on when they were not sure about cereal on the table or money for the rent.

Early in my years as a pastor I discovered the value of a passable singing voice and a memory bank numbering hundreds of hymns. Often a person in a hospital or a nursing home was too weak to engage in much conversation but quite ready to hear a favorite hymn. So I would ask, in the course of my pastoral calls, "Before I pray and go on my way, is there a favorite hymn you'd like me to sing for you?" Some would say, "I love them all. Choose one that you especially like," but more often folks would offer favorites of their own. I remember especially a great gentleman who was very near death. He had enjoyed success in business and community life and had recently endowed a chair in sacred music at a theological seminary. When I asked if he would like a hymn, he answered without hesitancy, "Sing, 'Jesus loves me! This I know.'" It had been a song of his childhood and one that had stayed with him through a long life of faithful discipleship. Now it was his song in the night, a song of transition from this world to the next.

Night has many definitions, as many as the varieties of human experience. Of the more than seven thousand hymns that Charles Wesley wrote, one of the abiding favorites is "Jesus, Lover of My Soul." Some say it is too sentimental. Perhaps they feel this way because they have never felt "the nearer waters roll" or wondered when "the storm of life" might be past. Or perhaps they simply are not inclined to so forthright a declaring of their emotions. No one knows for sure the circumstances that inspired Wesley's writing of the hymn, though several quite different stories have been offered. Perhaps the most significant insight is in the title Wesley first gave it: "In Times of Prayer and Temptation," which he abbreviated in later editions to "In Temptation." A soul wanting desperately to do right while in a storm of temptation needs a song. It is good to have a song for such a night.

Wesley's song for the soul struggling with temptation is a plea from a place of near helplessness. Another great soul who was nearly overwhelmed responded not with a plea but with a challenge into the teeth of the foe. Martin Luther, focal point of the Protestant Reformation, was at the darkest hour in his movement when at Coburg he wrote "A Mighty Fortress Is Our God." In it he declared that

> though this world, with devils filled,
> should threaten to undo us,
> we will not fear, for God hath willed
> his truth to triumph through us.

Luther was challenging not only armies and political powers but also hell itself. In a dark night, Luther got a song.

Sometimes, however, our nighttime songs hover perilously between hope and despair. Many of us remember Henry Wadsworth Longfellow for "The Song of Hiawatha" or "Paul Revere's Ride." But on Christmas Day of 1863, when America was at the height and depth of the Civil War, Longfellow wrote "Christmas Bells":

> I heard the bells on Christmas Day
> Their old, familiar carols play,
>   And wild and sweet
>   The words repeat
> Of peace on earth, good-will to men!

But then, "In despair I bowed my head; / 'There is no peace on earth,' I said." But then the insistent voice of faith rose up—"Then pealed the bells more loud and deep: / 'God is not dead, nor doth He sleep' "— so that Longfellow could conclude that "the world revolved from night to day" once again. Longfellow got a song in the night that persuaded him the day was coming. As it happened, the Civil War would not end until 1865, but the song sustained Longfellow then, just as it has sustained hundreds of thousands since then when they have wondered if we can ever expect peace on earth and universal goodwill.

But by now someone wants to contest a matter with me, and rightly so. You want to point out that many of the hymns you love best are songs of great joy, which must surely have been born in the very sunlight of religious experience. I agree. I think of them in every level of worship, from the stately exuberance of "Joyful, Joyful We Adore Thee" and "When Morning Gilds the Skies" to such rollicking revival songs as "O, Say But I'm Glad" and "I'm Going Higher Someday." My taste in hymns is broad enough that the whole repertoire of such sunlight hymns delights me.

So why then do I make a case for songs that are born in the night? To begin with, because the Christian faith begins in the night. Christ didn't come to our planet because it seemed a nice place for a thirty-three-year vacation but because our planet was in desperately bad straits and needed a redeeming visit. Christianity was born in the darkness of human need, not in the brilliance of humanity's achievements.

And what is true of our planet as a whole is more often than not true of individual experience. The macrocosm and the microcosm are consistent. Some years ago when I visited in a more-than-comfortable suburban home, the owner said, "I suspect I'm an exception to the rule. I didn't turn to Christ because I was in trouble but in a time when everything was going my way." As he spoke, I recalled the answer a very popular Catholic priest gave in the mid-twentieth century when a writer asked him the secret of the many conversions in which he had played a part. He explained that it was no skill of his own. Rather, people turned to God when they were at a point of loss or crisis in life: a broken marriage, a career reversal, the death of a loved one, a major illness.

All of which is to say that most of us hear better in the night. Or perhaps it is that there are fewer competing sounds in the night. If I may say so, I wonder if the shepherds would have heard as well if the choir had sung the *Gloria* at midday.

In other words, the issue is not entirely—perhaps not even primarily— the quality of the song but also the attentiveness and receptivity of the hearer. Christmas came when our planet was at night, and since its message is one of salvation, its music is always heard best when the listener is coping with some measure or quality of darkness.

That being so, don't despise the time of darkness, and for that matter don't embrace it either. Just listen carefully for the angels' song. It is good for every hour and every season. But it proves its truth best when it comes at night.

Study Questions

1. Share your favorite Christmas music and why it is so special to you.

2. What is meant by the phrase "the best songs come at night"?

3. How dark was the world into which Jesus was born? Give some examples.

4. How is the music of Advent different from other hymns?

5. What is different or unique about songs of the night?

6. Reflect on / discuss the author's statement that Christian faith begins in the night.

Prayer

Dear God, thank you for the special music of this Advent season. Help us not only enjoy it but also allow it to minister to us. Grant us a song in our hearts this season. Amen.

Focus for the Week

Continue your observance of Advent by paying attention to the special music of the season. Reflect on the images and messages of Advent songs. Listen to your favorite Advent music this week.

Wise Men
Follow a Star

Scripture: Read Matthew 2:1-11

Let me confess at the outset that I have no obvious qualifications for writing a definition of *wisdom* or of what constitutes a wise person. I could defend my brash effort by pointing out that there are sportswriters who can't throw a ball from left field to third base and music critics who can't carry a tune. But to define a *wise* man? Surely a person who takes on such an assignment needs some measurable qualifications.

I'm counting, however, not on any record of personal wisdom but on a story of some men who are the best-known wise men in human history, with a reputation that has won them a place in stories, legends, poetry, sermons, popular music, and opera. What I want to know is this: how is it that they hold such a unique and unparalleled position in the annals of wisdom?

Let me begin with what is for many people a very familiar story. You'll find the original in the first book of the New Testament, the Gospel of Matthew. Somewhere in "the east"—very likely in Persia—there was a team of men who were on a quest. The Bible calls them "wise men"; in our time they would probably fall somewhere between research scientists in a university and professional scholars in a political think tank. In our day, learned persons are almost always highly specialized, devoting themselves to quite esoteric areas of knowledge and research simply because the domain of knowledge has become so great that one can't hope to be a generalist. But in the ancient world, those who were learned generally took the whole realm of knowledge as their domain—mathematics, astronomy, economics, political science, logic, language, rhetoric, and the natural sciences.

Scholars in those times drew no sure line between astronomy and astrology. They were so taken with the wonders of the heavens that they felt that the movements of the stars influenced the conduct of life on the earth. The men in our story had determined by their research that a new king was to be born to the Jews. And right here, notice something very special about these men. They were not satisfied simply to get an idea and to release it to the world at large while they embarked on some other research project. Once they got the impression that a new king of the Jews was born or was about to be born, they set off on a long and quite perilous journey to see if they could find this new leader. Their learning had a demanding, insistent quality: *knowing* compelled *acting*. It was not enough to know that such a king existed; they must see him for themselves.

You may have noticed by now that I keep referring to these men without the defining adjective that now seems inseparably linked with them: *three*. The Bible doesn't give us any number. We speak of *three* wise men because they brought three gifts—gold, frankincense, and myrrh. This is a logical sort of deduction, so from this time forward in our story I will no longer avoid the familiar term.

Their inspiration and their guide was a *star*. But I suspect there would be some imprecision in following a star. That is, the area where a star seems brightest is not a pinpoint location. We're not surprised, therefore, that they did a quite logical thing: they went to the city of Jerusalem. After all, if you're looking for a king of the Jews, you would go to what had once been for Jews the capital city, Jerusalem, reasoning that if this people—who had been without a king for some six centuries—now had a king, he would be in the city they held politically and religiously sacred. When the wise men got to Jerusalem, they inquired, "Where is the child who has been born king of the Jews? For we observed his star at its rising, and have come to pay him homage" (Matthew 2:2).

Now if you don't mind, I'm going to speculate a bit. I think these wise men may possibly have lost their star somewhere along the way. Specifically, I wonder if they lost it when they got too logical and assumed that Jerusalem had to be the end of their journey. Where else, they might have reasoned, would you find a Jewish king if not in Jerusalem, and if not in the palace? So they went directly to King Herod, a man who was almost maniacally fearful of losing his throne. But Herod knew where to do research: he called upon the chief priests and scribes.

Of course, these Jewish scholars knew their Hebrew Scriptures very well. They knew that according to the prophet Micah their nation would someday have a great king who would be born in Bethlehem of Judea (Micah 5:2). As the wise men reconvened their journey, Matthew tells us, "there, ahead of them, went the star that they had seen at its rising." They followed it "until it stopped over the place where the child was. When they saw that the star had stopped, they were overwhelmed with joy" (Matthew 2:9-10). They had followed a star, and I think they had lost it. Now they had gotten hold of it again until at last it had come to rest at their destination. And the sight of that star, fulfilled, brought joy beyond measure. Those who are wise follow a star.

I suspect you realize that my little proverb is almost a contradiction within itself. It would make more sense if I were to say, "Those who are romantic follow a star," or perhaps "Dreamers follow a star." Those who claim to be wise ought to have their feet on the solid ground of dependable research. People who get stars in their eyes quite frequently stumble over some impediment in their pathway.

Think for a moment just how starstruck these wise men were. From our vantage point, twenty centuries later, in a world where Christianity is the largest single religion in the world, the wise men were—obviously—wise indeed. They were true visionaries, with judgment and insight beyond their time.

But consider how it was in their own day. They were looking for a new king of the Jews. *Why?* After all, who cared? Caesar was on the throne of the vast, dominating Roman Empire, while the Jews were a minority people within that empire—indeed, in many ways, one of the lesser minorities. Further, the Jews hadn't had a king of their own for some six centuries. And even when they had a king, they were seldom a power broker in the world of international politics. What difference would a king of the Jews make? Why would wise men—students of world politics operating in an eastern think tank—care about what was happening to a relatively small body of people who had been without political influence for so long that they wouldn't know how to handle it if it were given to them? Especially since they were a people with a religion that made them rather seclusive and that, at times, made it difficult for them to operate in the wider world of political affairs. So, as the wise men started their journey, it would seem that even if they found a new king of the Jews, he would be little more than an underling to the emperor in Rome. Why bother to cross a threatening desert and endure weeks of painful uncertainty to meet the new king of a rather tiny nation with no real government of its own? Could it be that they weren't so wise after all?

But you see, they were following a star. And the wisest of the wise follow a star. Of all the research specialists, astronomers, mathematicians, and government consultants who lived in the first century, these three anonymous wise men are by far the most widely known today, some twenty centuries later.

But be cautious. While it is true that wise men follow a star, so do a large number of irresponsible adventurers. I'm in a good position to know. I was a pastor for nearly forty years, many of those years in downtown churches. So many dreamers come to ministers with their stories, sometimes because they think that, as men and women of faith, we will be more likely to believe their ideas and sometimes because they feel that a minister is more willing to listen sympathetically. I've heard some wonderful, star-studded stories of inventions that never materialized, business ventures that never got to the bank, romances that never developed, and political movements that never got farther than a petition with fifty names. To say nothing of religious movements that promised to be the new Reformation and never got farther than a house meeting with three participants! I've seen enough ill-advised folks going after their star to make me properly skeptical of self-declared wise men and women.

But with that disclaimer I must go on to say that history is brilliantly lit up by those wise ones who *have* followed a star and who have re-shaped our human story by doing so. Several years ago a major American company in Cleveland, Ohio, published a fascinating advertisement in *Harper's* magazine. In it they pictured several people, each with a quotation that (to put it in the language of our present theme) argued against following a star. For instance, in 1899, Charles H. Duell, who was then commissioner of the United States Patent and Trademark Office, supposedly said, "Everything that can be invented has been invented." (I'm glad some computerwise person saw a star beyond Mr. Duell's vision.) And Grover Cleveland, twice president of the United States and a pretty savvy political visionary, said in 1905, "Sensible and responsible women do not want to vote." (Don't tell Hillary Clinton or Sarah Palin.) Robert Millikan was quite a dreamer in his own way, winning the Nobel Prize in physics in 1923. He is credited with saying, "There is no likelihood man can ever tap the power of the atom." The advertisement concluded, "There is no future in believing something can't be done. The future is in making it happen" ("The Future Isn't What It Used to Be," *Harper's* [November 1985]: 14). Those who have followed a star have known that for a long time.

At her best, the church has always had some great souls who followed a star. I regret that in some instances they have been forced out of the mainstream of their particular body or denomination. William Booth was a Methodist preacher in England for nine years, but he kept seeing a star—and the Lord knows he saw it in some strange places! He couldn't escape the idea that in God's eyes the last and the least of England's population, the poorest derelicts of society, had a future in this world and in the world to come. Almost all of us know something of what has happened to Booth's star. Today the movement he and his wife, Catherine, started—the Salvation Army—ministers in nearly ninety countries and colonies with more than eight thousand centers in the United States alone. For many people, it is the essence of all that is good about Christianity. The story is in some ways very simple: William and Catherine Booth saw a star, and they followed it. Yes, followed it through a desert as hopeless and trackless and unpromising as the original wise men knew.

A few years ago, my wife, Janet, and I stopped one vacation evening on the campus of Williams College in Massachusetts at a spot commemorating the Haystack Prayer Meeting. In 1806 a group of students from Williams College, overtaken by a thunderstorm, took shelter under a haystack during their prayer meeting. Out of the meeting that night they took a commitment that resulted in 1810 in the formation of the American Board of Commissioners for Foreign Missions—a body that many see as the beginning of the missionary vision in North America. Some must have seen them as unrealistic college students with dreams beyond their capacity. Today we know they were wise men, following a star, followed since by literally thousands of other visionaries, young and old.

I have a prejudiced outlook on life, which I'll express right here. I believe that the wisest men and women who follow their stars are those who see hope and prospect in human beings. They rarely win the prominence of newspapers or of history books by doing so, but under God they are the very carriers and caretakers of civilization. I'm speaking of those parents, teachers, grandparents, neighbors, clergy, and employers who can see the potential in other humans—perhaps especially those humans who are easily overlooked. Ask people in almost any field why they have succeeded and, inevitably, they will come around to naming someone who believed enough in their abilities or their possibilities to invest time, love, and encouragement. And yes, often money. Everything on our planet that is worthwhile would end in a generation if it were not for wise men and women who follow a star as they see that star in some human being.

And I hasten to add that the star is to be found not only in the young and their possibilities. Some of the greatest prospects can be found in people who have reached their middle years and have come to a fork in the road; or in some in retirement years who, like Grandma Moses, find their talent late or, like many an older person, have finally accumulated enough experience and wisdom to begin sharing it. Find a star in some human being, and who knows what brightness you may set loose in our world.

But if you're hoping to become a wise person, I must warn you that the wise man's journey is rife with disappointment and peril. That thoughtful and sometimes playful twentieth-century poet, W. H. Auden, imagined himself as one of the wise men and imagined their complaints about the weather (I think one would make such

35

complaints, traveling in that part of the world) and the dreary countryside (I venture the sameness got pretty tedious).

I wonder how often one of the wise men said, "Whose idea *was* this, anyway?" And how often did someone say, "Do you think we lost track of that star?" Some evenings, surely, one of them said, "I'm lonesome for my family. Do you think, perhaps, we should turn back?" Auden suggested that the one thing they knew for certain is that they were "three old sinners." I'll agree with Auden on that surmise because I think that here is one of the best evidences that we're wise, when we know that we're sinners. That's why we need the guidance of God's star.

You see, I suspect that no one has ever followed a star without sometimes wondering whether it was the right, the prudent, the sensible thing to do. Some nights even the brightest star is hidden in the clouds. And if that happens for enough consecutive nights, you may begin to wonder if there ever really was a star. Sometimes some folks will try, cautiously or broadside, to convince you that what has seemed to you a star is only a defect in your vision and that if you'd look at your star in the blazing good sense of daytime, you'd recognize as much.

No matter! God continues to throw grand stars into the landscape of our lives, and now and again, if we are fortunate and if we keep our spiritual antennae well-positioned, we catch our glimpse of one of those stars. Unfortunately, if our faith has been battered too many times or if we're unconscionably tired, we may shrug our shoulders, shake our heads, and go on our routine way.

But now and again, some of us will respond as did those ancient wise men. Seeing the star, we will be "overjoyed." In that exhilaration of faith and hope, we'll push aside our fears and what at other times we call our common sense, we'll pack up our energy, our dreams, and probably some of our money, and we'll set out to see where the star will lead us.

But just this special, further word: whatever other stars you follow, and wherever those stars may lead, be sure, please, to follow the star that leads to Bethlehem. Follow that star to Jesus Christ and to life eternal. It is the one star that you must not miss.

Study Questions

1. What is known about the wise men who followed the star?
2. What does it mean to follow a star? What type of people do it?
3. The church has a rich history of great souls who followed a star. Give some examples of these great Christians.
4. Share a time when you followed a star.
5. What lessons can we learn from the wise men?
6. Reflect on / discuss the important role of the wise men in the Christmas story.

Prayer

Dear God, thank you for throwing grand stars into the landscape of our lives. Help us follow the Star that leads to Bethlehem and to celebrate the wonders of this special season. Amen.

Focus for the Week

Continue your observance of Advent by seeking Jesus, just as the wise men did. Share the love of Jesus with others this week and assist others on their journey to see the King of Kings.

Christmas Lasts Longer Than You Think

Scripture: Read Luke 2:25-38

I am altogether sure that someone who is reading the title of this chapter wants to say to me, "You're absolutely right. We never take down our decorations until the middle of January, and we don't finish paying for the presents until the middle of September. And sometimes, not then."

I understand what you're saying, but it isn't what I have in mind. I'm thinking just now of two of my favorite people. They're not only two of my favorite people in the Bible—though that's where you'll find them—they're among my favorite people in all the world. The Lord willing, I want to meet them someday in heaven. Mind you, I'm not in a hurry to do so, but I do anticipate the day.

They were a man and a woman, but they weren't married. I don't even know that they knew each other. Not to the point of speaking to each other, that is. It's quite likely that they were familiar with each other's faces, habits, and reputations, but because they were male and female and because they lived in a culture where a man didn't speak to a woman in public—not even his own sister—these two could have seen each other in the marketplace, passed often on a village road, or seen each other on the outskirts of the place of worship, yet never have had a true conversation.

Now even though I've told you that these two are among my favorite people and that I look forward to meeting them in heaven, I have to confess that if I had met them in their lifetimes, I might not have paid attention to either of them. I think they were the sort of folks who easily could have been overlooked. The woman was very old, and there's every reason to think that the man, too, was in his later years. I suspect that, in the usual judgment of things, they were probably very ordinary looking. I like to think, as I look at some older people, that I can find a dozen stories in their faces, sometimes even a full novel. But I'm romanticizing when I think that way. If you had looked at these two people—looked at them, that is, in the hurried way that we often see people in the shopping mall or in passing traffic—you might not have seen anything in their faces that compelled even a second look.

But let me tell you more about these people. The man's name was Simeon. The Bible says that he was a righteous man, a devout man. When it comes to character, the Bible has high standards, so it doesn't use words like *devout* and *righteous* casually. He was also a great patriot. Now patriotism is fairly cheap in good times, if you're part of a conquering nation or of the controlling party. But this man was a patriot in Israel, a nation that hadn't had an extended period of independence for some six hundred years. It's hard to keep thinking well of your nation under such circumstances.

But there's more, much more, to Simeon's patriotism. Simeon believed in his nation because he believed that they were meant to bring a blessing to the whole human race. He was such a simple, pure idealist! His wasn't a triumphalist attitude that envisioned Israel ruling the world. Quite simply, he understood that God was going to send his

Messiah into the world for the blessing of all humankind, and Simeon longed to see that happen. Then, somehow, he got a wonderfully personal feeling about all of this: he sensed that the Holy Spirit had revealed that he, Simeon, wouldn't die until he had seen this visitation from God, this Messiah come to Israel and to the world.

Now let me be absolutely honest with you. Most of us would look pretty skeptically at a person with such a dream, or if you prefer, such a spiritual revelation. We might judge them to be quite harmless, but living, nevertheless, with a delusion. Some devout Jews had been expecting the Messiah for several centuries, which was admirable. But this particular kindly, older man walked through his days believing that the Holy Spirit had promised him that—of all things!—he would live until this long-awaited person had appeared.

Then one day, "guided by the Spirit," Simeon came into the Temple. Before long a young couple came in, a peasant couple, it was easy to see: modestly dressed, obviously people of the earth. They were carrying a young child. My son is a preacher, and a good one. My son also has a sense of humor. He asked me once, "How many couples do you think Simeon went up to before he found the right one?" Well, the Bible tells us that Simeon was led to this couple by the Holy Spirit, but still, my son may have a point. That is, I wonder if Simeon ever got impatient during the months or years of his waiting so that perhaps he asked—not necessarily some couple, but God—"Is this the one I've been waiting for?" Surely he must have gotten impatient at times, or tired of waiting, or perhaps even doubted the promise he had received.

No matter. Whatever doubts he may have had, or whatever indomitable faith drove him on, now the Spirit of God had led him to this young couple, this rather radiant teenage girl and this muscular, just-a-bit uneasy young man, a carpenter, a village handyman. Probably Simeon had noticed that these folks were poor. It wasn't simply their dress or their demeanor. It was that when they presented their baby to the priest, their offering was the smallest allowed by the Jewish law. It was the poor people's offering. Nevertheless, it was to this couple that Simeon knew he was led.

So Simeon took the baby in his arms. I wonder if Joseph and Mary thought it strange. It's one thing, after all, for a stranger to approach a couple, smile at the baby, perhaps even make some supposedly cute sounds to get the baby to smile, ask about its age and its name, then move on. But actually to *take* the baby from the parents for a moment? I'm told that people sometimes do strange things as they grow older (I wouldn't know, of course), but to take an infant from a couple, just like that?

But old Simeon had just begun. He wasn't content simply to hold the child in his arms. Now he made a speech. Well, in truth, a prayer, but a speech was written into it, a declaration for the world to hear. He looked up to heaven and said, "Now I can die! I can die in peace, because my life is fulfilled. I have seen your salvation, / which you have prepared in the presence of all peoples, / a light for revelation to the Gentiles / and for glory to your people Israel" (Luke 2:30-32, adapted).

What a remarkable human being this Simeon was! He had lived a long life, and he had held to a grand dream: that God would someday send a Savior to Israel and that this person would bless not only Israel but Gentiles as well. That is, that God was about to send a blessing to the whole human race. Because, you see, Simeon's people divided the human race into two groups—Jews and Gentiles—and Simeon dared to say that God was going to bless them both; specifically, God was going to bless the whole human race, and by way of this child that Simeon was at that moment holding in his arms!

At this point in the happenings, someone else was edging into the scene, a woman named Anna. She was at least eighty-four years old, which is a bit of a story in itself in a world where life expectancy was roughly half that. She had married, no doubt as a teenager as was the custom in her culture, but had been widowed just seven years later and had now survived as a widow for some sixty years. This, too, was quite an accomplishment. In that world and time, a widow had to be supported by the closest male relative, whether a brother, a brother-in-law, a father, or a son. We don't know how Anna managed, except that we're told that she was a prophet.

Being a prophet was a rather risky enterprise. Prophets didn't have employers or a pension program. They were freelancers, dependent on the response and trust of the people who heard them or consulted them. We can't know for sure what Anna's work as a prophet entailed, but I suspect she spoke on occasion to gatherings that would listen to her, and probably she ministered at a personal level to people who sought her counsel and strength. When the Gospel of Luke tells us that she did a great deal of fasting, a cynical observer might conclude that probably at times she had little choice: her meager income made fasting a necessity!

As the years went by, however, her life took a more concentrated turn. The Bible says that she "never left the temple but worshiped there with fasting and prayer night and day" (Luke 2:37). Anna had a focus on her life that all but consumed her. When she saw the baby Jesus, that focus found its meaning. She "began to praise God and to speak about the child to all who were looking for the redemption of Jerusalem" (Luke 2:38).

It must have been quite a scene on that otherwise quiet day when the baby Jesus was presented in the Temple for the rite of purification. As far as we know, no extended family was present for the event; it was apparently just Joseph and Mary and Jesus, performing a stated ritual of their Jewish faith. But an old man, Simeon, had gotten an early news release that the answer to Israel's prayers was to appear in the Temple that day. And an old woman named Anna, who spent all her time in prayer and fasting, suddenly became greatly energized so that she "praised God." As I think of the kind of woman Anna must have been, I have a feeling that she became pretty audible. Then she began buttonholing every thoughtful soul she could find so she could tell them the good news: this was the child who would bring redemption!

This all happened roughly six weeks after the first Christmas. Christmas wasn't over the night Jesus was born. It didn't end when the shepherds came to the manger to see the child wrapped in swaddling clothes. Christmas had just begun.

But back to those two people who were present in the Temple that day, Simeon and Anna. Perhaps you noticed something rather interesting about them, that is, about the way they responded to seeing Jesus. When Simeon saw the child, his first words were, "Now I'm ready to die!" His words, in their complete form, are sung in Christian festivals all over the world. They are usually identified by their Latin translation: *Nunc dimittis.* That is, "Now dismiss us." Simeon experienced Christmas and said, "Now it's time to go. I'm ready to die." Anna, on the other hand, saw the Christ Child and began to tell everyone in reach about this child who would bring redemption.

Now, I know very well what some of you are thinking at this point. You want to say that this response is really quite predictable. These two people were just personality types. And some would go further, reducing the story to some broad, general differences—at least, as generally perceived—between men and women: men are more quiet and introspective and women are more vocal, so give these two people the same momentous event and the man turns introspective and says he's ready to die, and the woman turns social and wants to talk. It figures, someone might say.

And I'll concede the point. Not necessarily as a difference between men and women, because there are different kinds of men and different kinds of women. I remember a plane trip many years ago when I was sitting next to a man who talked so incessantly that I began to think that perhaps a plane crash wasn't too bad an idea as long as it ended this monologue. There are differences between people, whether male or female.

But what I want to say, clearly and emphatically, is this: Simeon and Anna were both right. Think first about Anna. When the Lord Jesus Christ came to our planet, it was such good news that those who experience his coming want to tell others about it. No wonder then that we have a spiritual that declares, "Go, tell it on the mountain, / that Jesus Christ is born." That was Anna's mood, and she was right. She had the Christmas spirit.

But Simeon was right too. Because since Jesus Christ came to our planet, bringing with him God's eternal life, we're ready to die. This part of the Christmas story wasn't finished until thirty-three years later, at the first Easter, but it began of course in the Bethlehem manger. Now that Jesus has been born, I can die, because there's nothing more to worry about if I trust in him.

So Simeon was right too. Anna and Simeon were *both* right.

That's what I mean when I say that Christmas lasts longer than you think. Perhaps one of the reasons so many people feel a bit melancholy at Christmastime is because they see Christmas as a once-a-year event, except for paying the bills and taking down the decorations, when in truth Christmas is an *eternal* event. It began for our universe when our Lord was born in Bethlehem, and it begins for any of us when we accept the Lord of Bethlehem and Calvary as the Lord of our lives. And when we so accept him, we're ready to live or ready to die.

The Apostle Paul got the point very well—so well, that it left him in a wonderful quandary. He tells about it in a letter to one of his favorite congregations, in Philippi. At the time, he was in prison. He had plenty of time there to contemplate what life was all about. As he did so, he said that he was hard-pressed as to what he wanted. On one hand, he wanted to keep on living so he could preach and teach, winning people to Christ and leading them deeper in their faith. But on the other hand, he would like to die, so he could be with his Lord. It was a hard choice, he said, because both possibilities were so attractive.

So it is that I find the best of the Christmas spirit in Anna and Simeon and in Paul's later words about what life and eternity meant to him. In fact, I feel that the better we grasp this full message of Christmas, the more we will feel as Paul did. We're ready to live. I mean *really* live—not just exist, not putting one dogged day after another, but grasping life for all it's worth. Jesus Christ does that to life. But because of Christmas, we're also ready to die. Ultimately, I think we ought to come out where Paul did. He decided that he ought to go on living, to do the work God had called him to do. But if God decided to issue his exit papers, Paul was ready to die.

So I'm back where I started. Simeon and Anna were both right. And as we pass Christmas Day, I hope you'll remember that *Christmas has just begun*. Because our Lord has come to this planet, and because if you've accepted him as Lord of life, then you can make both Anna and Simeon your patron saints. You're ready to live, really living, loving Christ, loving life, loving people. And you're ready to die.

That makes Christmas a really big deal, doesn't it? It's a shame if we end Christmas too soon and miss opening the rest of the grand package. Because on December 25, Christmas has just begun.

Study Questions

1. Name one of your favorite people in the Bible. Why is this person a favorite?
2. What is known about Simeon?
3. Reflect on / discuss why Christmas really just *begins* on December 25.

4. Share what the Bible tells us of Anna. What was her role in the Christmas story?
5. How did both Simeon and Anna respond to seeing Jesus?
6. Explain why Simeon and Anna were both right.

Prayer

Dear God, thank you for pioneers of faith like Simeon and Anna. Help us remember that Christmas is not a once-a-year event. May we enjoy the gifts of Christmas all year long. Amen.

Focus for the Week

Conclude your observance of Advent by preparing your heart and soul for Christmas. Share the joy of this season with others and continue to celebrate the meaning of Christmas throughout the year.